# The Neighbor Out of Sound

# The Neighbor Out of Sound

## Jake Marmer

Sheep Meadow Press
Rhinebeck, New York

Designed and typeset by Sheep Meadow Press
Distributed by The University Press of New England


Cover art: Lola Migas and Ryan Diaz *Chromapoems—I have a Dream*


Library of Congress Cataloging-in-Publication Data

Names: Marmer, Jake, author.
Title: The neighbor out of sound / Jake Marmer.
Description: Rhinebeck, New York : Sheep Meadow Press, 2018.
Identifiers: LCCN 2018016757 | ISBN 9781937679781 (pbk.)
Classification: LCC PS3613.A76664 A6 2018 | DDC 811/.6--dc23
LC record available at https://lccn.loc.gov/2018016757


All inquiries and permission requests should be addressed to the publisher:


Sheep Meadow Press
PO Box 84
Rhinebeck, NY 12572

# ACKNOWLEDGEMENTS & THANKS

\*

I would like to thank Rachel Tzvia Back and Hank Lazer for reading the manuscript and offering their generous and valuable feedback. Much gratitude to Jerome Rothenberg for his early guidance on the nigun poems, and suggestion to transform footnotes into poetics. Thank you to Adeena Karasick, Charles Bernstein, Al Filreis, and Frank London for their support, warmth, and inspiration. Thank you to Stanley Moss, a visionary editor and poet. Thank you to Shoshana, and to Lev & Ora, as ever.

\*

Below are some of the publications where these poems have first appeared. Much gratitude to the editors.

*Current Musicology*: "Painters' Nigun," "À Rebours," "Root-Note Nigun," "Nigun for Cecil Taylor" (originally, "Cecil's Scarecrow Nigun").

*The Forward*: "Everywhere," "The Robe," and "One Year Plan."

*Ilanot Review*: "Checkers in Reverse," (originally, "Translation as Recipe" and "Poddvaki").

*The Materialist*: "Lunch Break Reflections."

*Moment Magazine*: "3 AM Nigun."

*Philadelphia Supplement*: "Change of Weather."

*Poems and Poetics*: "The Laws of Returning Lost Objects."

*Poet's Quest For God Anthology* (UK): "Ingress" (originally, "Loophole").

*Schlemiel Theory*: "Same Ass But View Sideways," "Banya," (originally, "Public Bathhouse,") "Memoir."

*Tablet Magazine*: "Adding It Up."

*The Word Hotel*: "Pinafore Dream" and "The Second Place."

# TABLE OF CONTENTS

The Bells a Winter Night
Bearing the Neighbor out of Sound
That never did alight

**-Emily Dickinson**


the old jew strains at his gabardine
  it parts for him
  his spirit rushes up the mountainside
  & meets an eagle
  no an iggle […]
& the iggle lifts him
  like an elevator
  to a safe place above the sunrise
  there gives a song to him
  the Baal Shem's song
  repeated without words for centuries
  "hey heya heya" but translates it
  as "yuh-buh-buh-buh-buh-buh-bum"

**-Jerome Rothenberg**


There is no quiet prayer. Because there is anxiety about the authenticity of the prayer. And I'm not the one who can decide about authenticity of the prayer. Only the other one can decide. And the other one is just a question mark.

**- Jacques Derrida**

# The Neighbor Out of Sound

*

*Nigun is a traditional Hasidic chant, usually wordless.*

*It is a thick, dense place. It is a way of echo-locating yourself in the void. Or is it a form of summoning what George Quasha called the "altered state of listening"?*

*The chant often becomes the lever of the ritual it is associated with — wedding ceremony, holiday gathering, Talmud study, candle-lighting, or pilgrimage to a mystic.*

*These next few poems attempt to reach a similar state of mind, the nigun-head, through words.*

*

## Nigun: Methodology

If you don't know how
    stick your head in a well
start talking, lowering

word stems
shaved antidotal
edge of the tessitura

echoes
will stretch
your voice
    into a song

your shadow
into a myth

will stretch till you can't
tell between thinking and listening

## Painters' Nigun

*On hearing Frank London's H.W.N.*


this is a song of people painting walls
walls of a shul that doesn't exist

the song of paint rolls upwards
            pulled by other gravities

the inanimate painted
with breath
            breathes
            as it is said:
"living words"

painting walls on the scaffolding of a drum solo
of fists banging a table, palms banging
the table, it is real –
but the solo is a thought, a draft
sweeping across the shul that doesn't exist

the sound rises like an animal, walks
                        moving its burden
to the pit
            built for the chanters
as it is said "from the depth…"

this song commemorates what
has never happened
but the paint the paint
rolls like walls rolls like sea

sound rising
                mercurially

# Root-Note Nigun

this nigun is about a stick figure
a two-bone abstraction, solitary root
note, resounding its stripped chorus –

this nigun is about a scratch,
loose nerve, bristle dropped
into a legendary painting,
an epic ball of flesh and color

this nigun knows there must've been
a mistake and mumbles
all it ever knows to mumble
– "I exist" – "I exist" – "I exist" –
note bent in and out of the question

this nigun is about a stick figure
imagining it could change its fate
by lifting its stick-figure hands
                                    heavenward

# 3 AM Nigun

*for Shana*

lullaby's every heave
another tractate
on slowing down, peeling –

each note, a pit
collapsed prayer

lullaby's underside,
       hymn to darkness
of the dream's reaffirmed primacy:

sleep no longer a goal but a side-effect

two silences rise on each side of you
amplifying shadows of possession –

family of three – the dream of us
like the never-thickening liquid
all night poured in
and out of the bedroom's cup

## Amphibian Nigun

time hacked, piled
like slabs of ice
muddy myth-stairs

thought in its precise dimensions, all but one –
isn't that music?

obsession, as a form of ascent

cold ripples
melt the traces of the face
endless failure
to reach surface

for a minute you remember
the world at the bottom of the song

peopled with pulsating eyes
textual beards –

and when you pick up your head and ask for a drink
someone shows you to the ocean
says, welcome to your new life
under the water

# Nigun for Cecil Taylor

this nigun is a scarecrow

in your old coat & hat
looks a bit like you

scrap prophecy
on a stick –

to sing it is to acknowledge
the arc: both hands
speaking at once –
extremities of solitude

melody's oblivion pounded into lint

to sing it is to possess
through resemblance

the way we imagine a being
that resembles time
imagine to possess

freshly unknotted
we dissipate
into the scarecrow nigun –
      victorious,
           creaking guardian

in a field of pure color

## À Rebours

this nigun is an erasure

the way other songs reach into you
      this one retreats, taking with
            all that seemed nailed to the floor

cinematic in its reel

you may find yourself humming its residue

*

*I knew nothing about my ethnic origins until I was eight. We never spoke about it. One day, I was singing a little song I learned from friends in my Soviet elementary school. Papa sat me down: it's about this word, repeated in the song's chorus. Not a nice way of referring to Jews. Also: we're Jews.*

*The song started out like this:*

> *if the faucet got no water*
> *it's cause Yids have drank it*

*I know that every Russian Jew of my generation is familiar with this song.*

*Before I was eight, without being able to name the reference, I nevertheless sensed an undercurrent of intimations, the flurry of off-notes I came to know and later placed in my ancestral scale. Perhaps for that reason, when, as a teenager in America, I started piecing together the language of Jewish praxis and its abandonment, Yiddishkeit became alive to me as a poetics.*

*The next segment further explores these stolen waters, this mirage of a scale.*

*

# Sermon Over the Empty Dishwasher

Someone left the interpretation machine running
and it's the hungriest motherfucker
in the manifest world
I watch the tubes choke on plain air
its dry-heaving rhythm, the secret life
of our to and fro

Broke with nomadics. I sit
scribing the reciprocator, what else
can I feed it but obsession with concealment,
if I miss a tone the ladder will fall on the nest
of oneness, or fall out, or to the side,
in any case, epistles
will no longer fit on the stick, then what –

I am not as solo as it may sound:
people we both know visit, and daily
I still put my head in the cosmic mouth –
the circus awarded me
with a new dishwasher
as my holy uncle Stanislav Stasis
predicted

# Ingress

*Said Rabbi Ashi: On Sabbath, lying on a straw bed, you must not move straw with your hand, yet you may move it with your body.*

-Babylonian Talmud, Sabbath 50A

If you must move
that which can't be touched
move it
touching it
in a way no one would ever think of touching it.

What can't be imagined
bypasses reality,
then swallows it, from within.

When no word can describe what you're doing
you can get as close as you like –
and that's the secret of closeness
to the center
        of the Great Untouchable
    moving
near you like an old bird
moving straight
into your Talmudic glove
set at the gaping mouth
of the loophole.

## Shalom Aleichem: A Remix

peace to you glamorous angels dressed in fractured mirrors of grammar

peace to you eight-headed angels of cosmic immigration anxiety,
there's nowhere to go

come in peace angels whose celestial ears are sprouting webs of vacuum

come in peace flute playing angels of lemons for breakfast

bless me overloaded midnight distraction angels of avoided answers

bless me medicinal exegetic angels who will not stop arguing
not even if god herself

                                                     drops the mic

go in peace purple haired angels who fell off the recycling truck
and claim ownership

                                      of the very idea of falling

go in peace internal monologue angels of bad puns, pickled orgasm,
and ancestral, grafted

                                    desire to be, suddenly, angelic

# New Shabbes Hymn for Lovers & Partners

*Commissioned by Graham Parker for Adam Benson*

*Freely adapted from Eishet Chayil [Woman of Valor], Book of Proverbs (31:10-31)[1]*

my brave lover, who can find
me in my tangle of being –
precious –
my heart trusts itself
immersed in your beauty

you find me in my goodness and darkness
all of our days
weave me as ancients
wove prayer
shawls – unafraid
of the handiwork

like a sail
across a painting,
you rename distances
into hope

arising in the night
you inscribe my hunger
as law –
may it endure

a field
of forces and dreams we're
nourished by touch
and wine

---

[1] Poetic procedure used here is derived from Jerome Rothenberg's notions of "total translation." The original hymn is traditionally sung by a husband to his wife on the Sabbath eve; propelling the text forward, so as to open it to include all genders, all marriages, and to transcend fixed roles, was Graham's commission, and the point of departure for this composition.

15

walking in strength
flexing your grip
on the world we're creating
naming it
good –

nightlight, fragility, you
stretch your hands towards
your thought towards
our need, stretch it
upward

i know nothing about the snow but its beauty

you're scarlet
over my scars

scarlet poetry
scarlet sculpture

we're always at the gate –
unknowable
and older than the ground we stand on

you flow with strength and dignity
and laugh with abandon

you open your
body with wisdom
your tongue
is my kindness

blessing our wanderings,

you rise the way stars rise
the way bread rises, flowers –

in praise —

and i rise for you
as my words do
as my soul rises

the world is filled with radiance
but you're from beyond this world

words entangle themselves
sound stuck in the throat
but my awe
is my truest praise

## Pinafore Dream

the dream says: no images
but inside-things –
walk the shadow of shortcuts
      the mind is held by
what the Talmud calls "olive-sized" –
smallest acceptable
      modicum
      of facts, space, action
to count as occurrence –
to count as another feather –
stuck in the lapel
of the man of many peeling passports:

Referent
      Referrentovich

ominous root at lunchtime
still in bed, still got bounce, rotting or not –
whole family huddles, listening intently to his every growl
respectful because well-bred:
will squeeze the nose with two fingers while sneezing!
so as not to distract
the audience –
the class, as it were,
in session: you can hear the pin drop
and sure enough, it does

rain of pins

## Neither Adam

I'm birthing
myself
a stilt
thought turned
limb
no excruciating pain
nor pleasure
deep sleep
fathers me
unto me

## The Law of Returning Lost Objects

when is an object considered lost?
when the owner relinquishes the hope of finding it

when is an object considered lost?
the hope of finding apples
that tumbled out of the basket
                 date cakes that crumbled
                         dollar bills flying down the street
is not considered hope
desire for restitution no longer
has an object that can be perceived as whole
consciousness cannot wrap
around it as it does around experience

items' identity is that of scattering

the person who falls
upon the loss
is the new owner, as it is said:

if you fall upon scattered money it is yours
if you fall upon a scattered thought it is now your thought
scattered memory and the lost image become your possession

you're now in possession
of a memory that belonged to another
you're possessed in the image –
possessed with words that aren't your words
possessed with names no one has given you

when is an object considered lost?
when there're no identifying marks
money, for instance, got no memory
of the lost owner
and neither does language –
battle of fingerprints –

crooked sign on the old photograph spells
*ze shaar tzadikim yavou bo*
"this is the gate the righteous come through"
says
"welcome
our rebbe our teacher"
not much of a gate –
more of a hole in torn posters –
grime, dazed passersby –
the gate was collapsing even before it was lost
and if you wonder about the lost
righteousness, repeat
the word it till it comes
loose in your mouth
"righteousness"
till your teeth start rotting with sound you're
coming into possession of righteousness
you're trying to welcome
it is ravishing your mouth

the words are now yours and what's there to do
with words "the rebbe the teacher"
they're possessing you
they're impossible words
you'd like to return them
but the hope has been relinquished
you are now in possession

you lay on top of somebody's
lost words that fell near the gate
of righteousness
or else the gate falls on you as you're trying to pass
for a word yourself
trying to pass for the word "teacher"

collapsed gate of righteousness welcomes
all those returning
lost objects
a ritual
of fulfillment
of the positive commandment
of minding the aperture curating an exhibition or simply nailing
photographs to the wall

this dream cannot be mediated
but accepts your findings
you're no longer the owner of these losses
you're free to become a rabbi a teacher a curator
you may be welcomed at an altogether separate gate
publicized as a commandment
and scattered in the way all knowledge scatters
and the law of returning lost objects
will continue to apply

## Baal Shem's Teaching

Suddenly I remember Baal Shem's
teaching of misdirected prayers that never
ascend but bumble around crowding us all
       *that's because the misdirected ones are still alive!*
I say, thinking of all of the poems
I half-mumbled and let go of

the mangled name strains
gazing at the bend

what comes around bends the other way

you're my misdirected prayer

## 28 Colors

you were recently born
and don't know it
you've got 28 colors
                of panic
one day these will become
divine names you'll master
and stuff into amulets
you'll spray their chant-like dust
across hurting textual bodies

can't borrow that kind of a god
inasmuch as you can't borrow
an essence
or the idea of light

## Letter

"Losing faith is losing language"
writes David Meltzer
and: "the ritual means as long
as the words mean"
what I see
is that loss of faith
      *is*
a language
each unlinked chain of meaning
a letter
of some unsounded alphabet, new glyph
laid across the erogenous zone
of the ritual

# Reflex

Sometimes late at night in bed we talk like very pious Jews –
fractured mix of languages and accents and rhetoric

no recourse to compromise –
we play members of opposing sects, holy, disdainful,
and don't even laugh at our little banter

for it all flows so naturally
at night, across some dark mirror

memories
less parody than reflex

*2013/2017*

## Master of Return

I didn't wake up that morning with light in my mouth.
There was no smoking wreckage, a promise
or the big moment to tell my children about.

I remember learning that I've become a Master of Return.

Remember the pleasure of drowning
in the language I didn't understand
but could read, watching my thoughts released
into a more pure, sonic self. I felt God was hearing –
did I really believe or simply set my thoughts
upwards?

It didn't matter that I was returning
to a past
            wholly imagined,
A life I had not lived.
Myth and autobiography overlap
extemporaneously.

All reasons & explanations come back
to loneliness –
and I don't mean the lack
of companionship but the other kind – music
is how this loneliness gets across. Mind turns fire.

When the feeling left me it left me empty though
the reward for keeping the laws
            was the sweetness of release –

In all of these years, never
have I come closer to the point of my original turning
to total undoing of it all
than I am today –

I've been erasing my way
back to my origins: am I not, then, still
a Master of Return?

# Forefather

*"Go forth from your land…"*


command's doubling –
*lech lecha*
 "go forth" "going, go" "go into yourself"
like an echo
of footsteps across the text

every new repetition
another threshold
of self, the double, cracked mirror,
straining the nail of consonance
a busted etymology

echo –
this text's true protagonist

*


the compass
spins like a roulette

# Adding It Up

*"Gematria … interpretive freedom gone mad"*
*-Harold Bloom*

I have this relative, a young guy. Call him Gematria. Not *a* gematria, but Gematria with a capital G because that's his first name. Last name's Woodpecker. Rabbi Gematria Woodpecker, yes. Anytime we see each other at another family gathering, before I even wash my fingertips there's already an equation waiting for me at the table. Something adds up immediately! Gematria is a mystical thing: numbers behind letters that make up the words this universe is made of. A great cosmic abacus that takes into account not only causes and effects but all sorts of other variables (which, by the way, is precisely why effects don't add up to causes – a separate conversation). It is the world's wiring, and the guy's tonguing the naked plug. If you add "Jake" and "the shaking ladder" you get "rose" which is your wife, Shoshana, how's it going…? Subtract "bird" from "Jake and his hat" and you get the "blessing for the downtrodden," am I right or what? Of course he is right. The issue is the look that he gets as he busts these gematrias out. His three robes, the immaculate fringes, the breastplate – as if they're not even there. He's just grinning like one of those middle-aged guys who live for their puns. Plus, remember, he's a Woodpecker – he'll drill a hole in your head. If you don't have the brakes, don't start counting. Then again: we have nothing to say to each other, it's always awkward – what else has he got up his sleeve? I've been attracted to puns myself. If I too spent all my lunch-breaks communing with the chariot, if my Hebrew was much better, maybe I'd be gematrying all day long just like him. Come to think, would've been nice to spice up the conversation at this table we're sharing where I have nothing to say, and overall, aside from a few dead-end jokes, sprinkling of anecdotes, and the obligatory didactic thing, there's just not a whole lot happening for me, not a whole lot going on at all…

# Lines for Yom Kippur 5774

I would like to apologize to language for all of the misdirected syllables
for overdoing it – I thought that jamming was the thing of the past
I am sorry for the midnight refrigerator euphoria
masked as neo-entheogenics
forgive me the books
of Russian poets I shoved in the storage unit, it is dark & sinister
and for the sack of discomfort lugged and wrought and spread like wares –
I apologize to all Americans for consuming your words
they were so cold and unwanted
sorry about my rudimentary grill of foreignness
and its singed offering

# 4 Cups Midrash

*"In with wine, out with secrets"*
-Babylonian Talmud, Eruvin 65a


….so that your ideological donkey
stays stoned at the truth-trough

walk
walk through Babylon
on your own wobbly feet

## Wrench

On my 34th birthday
stayed at home all day
my son, sick, asleep
held him on the couch
tore myself from the book for a moment
to watch his face
"should do THAT more often"
same virus that got him coursing now through my own system
wife, asleep next to us, propping
her big pregnant belly on the pillows
back to the book
floated in and out of my body, as Ginsberg
had it, "a new Jewish kind of Yoga"
what went wrong with the garbage
disposal? our new sink full, stagnant, ill-smelling
like some domesticated overgrown pond
       was shabbes and as ordained
we rested
and when it ended
I took out my new wrench stuck it up the insinkerator
shaking stiffly then more vigorously, though still skeptical
I know nothing of objects that surround me
something gave way –
adulterating itself with gook and soap, the water
swirled and tumbled down
like a miniature self-imploding tornado

# Everywhere

Almost three years old, on the toilet
he says: god
is everywhere
but you can't see him, papa;
    the thing we fought for
    came back to bite us –
which is to say, yes, alright Jewish daycare
and the four under-slept queens that reign over it
but boy, the rhetoric? naming it?

in his time
my own papa said mysteriously:
the universe
has been around since
always
(and I'm crunching Ukrainian leaves
underfoot
trying to *feel* it)

later, my son & I in the shower,
I ask: but what is god? does it do anything?
as it occurs to me, I'm not asking this
expecting a party trick
but with that maybe-feeling one later gets embarrassed about
and as the water cascades over us
comes the verdict:
- says hi    says hi to everything

## The Third Alternative

"there're things that aren't imaginary
or real,

        papa – "
my son greets me, as I direct his steps
towards the toothbrush
"y'know what ah mean?"
he says, with the sort of an accent he surely didn't pick up at home
we're both shirtless, half-asleep
everything is blurry

and as we stand there, I assess the impossible
third alternative –

*neither imaginary nor real*

my neck starts to sweat –
as he clarifies:
"like toys, y'know? my monkey
or the bear with the menorah sweater?
they're not imaginary
but not real, either"

## The Rooster

I tell all sorts of little stories to my kids at night – all true things that really happened and by now they've asked for this particular one so often, it grew in weight, developed, you could say, scales of a formative myth of my selfhood.

Personally, I don't understand why. I think it's a terribly uninformative story to be remembered by.

When I was a kid, my parents and I lived in a one-room apartment. We moved around a bunch, too, but all of those places had only one room. And a kitchen. So I used to stay with grandparents a lot. They had their own house, on a street named after Caucasian Mountains, which I've seen on a map of the Soviet Union that hung in our classroom.

One morning, I was walking to school from my grandparents. It was a fifteen minute walk, and the cracked asphalt road was interrupted only once with a little park – but not the sort of a pleasant, civilized park you might be thinking of – more of a tree-filled Ukrainian emptiness. A wilderness perhaps?

The house before this wilderness had black sour cherry trees outside of it, and some hens pecking near the fence. There was also a big white rooster hanging around. I looked at the rooster closely, and before I knew it, our eyes locked: then, he bent his head down and charged towards me. I ran - for a long time without turning back. I still remember the backpack banging against my back.

The next day, I walked on the other side of the street, cautiously glancing at the house with cherry trees. I could swear I didn't mean to make eye contact with the rooster, but somehow I did – it's as if he's been waiting for it – and again, he charged towards me, and I ran.

The weeks that followed were tense and filled with fear. Once, finally, I realized that I had not seen the rooster for a few days. Then, a few more days went by. And a few more.

I finally told my father everything that transpired and asked him where the rooster went:
"The soup pot!" he said, knowingly.

## Writing Prompt for a Young Parent

When your kids are sick, really sick, let them into your bed.
Let them cough and drool on your pillow.
In the morning, inhale the pillow's worth of their sweet bad breath, and
their pain and terror intensified by sickness –
the terror you must have been the source of –
threats and discipline and compulsion
the puddle of language they will find their hopes inscribed in
you'll learn nothing about empathy or parenting
but the gates of your own childhood will burst open
as their dream-cough starts ripping through you
like a rogue plough, upturning words
in counterpoint to everything rationed
rational, and orderly.

# Lullaby

thoughts—dry branches—
I repeat, silently and obsessively, sitting, sitting in front of the crib
against the endless crying my soothing voice
like dog piss at Niagara
for 20 seconds I am not a parent
in and out of my body
in and out of circumstances of my identity
the burning
thoughts I won't allow myself to articulate
they're dry branches and burn
along with everything surrounding them
shadows of crib's slats
on my arms
I count up
and down, don't sing, shush
with a regularity, in—
creasing intervals   to slither out of the room
this is not a prayer nor plea nor family record—
and the scroll I imagine these words hanging on
lullaby's offal is what it's made of

## The Deck

every few years when it snowed really hard in New York
someone would inevitably comment: this is nothing for you, right?
you people are used to much heavier stuff—
but the truth is that the provincial town I come from—
deep in the steppes of Ukraine—was not big on winter
in fact it never snowed: when the weather turned
and clouds got heavy, what fell from the skies was not snow
but playing cards, very small denominations,
cards meant for losing,
cards that some angry Slavic god emptied out on his people,
cards that quivered, landing
on men's shoulders like epaulettes of ignobility

if you want to know, it wasn't very different
from what goes down in your Atlantic city, not altogether unlike
midtown streets littered with the same bad cards, one of which
I've just turned over, for your reading pleasure

## Loosening

the dream loosens its tie
stares down at the mirror—
the mirror pokes the back
of the dream's head—badly shaven
"at least no wires coming out
of the cuts" the dream mumbles
into a glass as if to summon water
or beer but there're only echoes
filling the cup, each echo carrying its own
resemblance to emptiness
the dream breathes life
into the echoes
—nothing happens—
the dream loosens its tie
every morning it wakes up with tightness in its throat

## Portrait

she starts crying
& drains my glass
her own glass untouched
half-full

## All Things You Could Be By Now

in my dream, I was hanging out with John Zorn
and although I knew it was him for certain
in the dream he looked like my mother-in-law –
       Hassidic woman from Brooklyn –
who phoned responding to the ad
about the dog-leash Zorn was selling?
I thought he'd be happy – he seemed pleased –
the customer was on the way up in the elevator
when it occurred to me: "there's no dog here"
and has never been one
whose leash was it
whose leash was it

# Goldberg Agitations

*for Ben Goldberg*

"*Man, I'm sorry, and I'm sure its just a personal thing of some kind, but, while I have never found a doorway into your music, as brilliant a musician and artist as you obviously are, this trio recording actually drove me away. Having listened to fragments of four selections, I actually became agitated. That may be a sign of successful art, but it plays hell on the commerce.*"

- festival's organizer's letter to Ben Goldberg, 5/31/2016

Man, I'm sorry I'm agitated because the zipper
of my mind has been open all evening and I've been talking
to people, people who think
in fragmented bird silences

my agitation is thick as honey
and I can't tell between love, polyphony,
and the thing polyphony is short for –
as is love –

man, this music drove me away towards
the place where I am no longer
an existential recycling bin
I'm sorry and agitated

and it's all fragments, these four selections,
as I am, and this plays hell on
metaphysics and commerce
must be a personal thing of some kind

# Alternatives to Nostalgia

*New Klezmer Trio*


to walk backwards into
something resembling light
      light shredding at your sides, to walk
backwards into mud, primordial mud
with something like fire
in your voice, to walk
into puddles of fire feeling
as manic as the black light illuminating
the walk backwards
into time
walk across the rear view mirror
through something resembling time

# Maestro

*For Jose Kozer*

the poet dances and talks about money

the poet plays variations on a bathroom joke

the poet starts to read    not a single word of English
the fugue state is all mine

But I see the raw form, the melody:
      apologetic half-step
      instead of the bow

the poet drinks from the plastic bottle
jokes about getting
paid   he reads a poem about his wife
in a language I don't understand
but he points to his eyes, points to the tip
of his head and I recognize
the word which must mean "circular" it is said twice
a flurry of apologetic half-steps
her name, Jerusalem, her name again, then
the final couplet – he conducts it
with one hand, as if dismissing
      an orchestra

## Call and Responsa

Newborn / sleep deprivation
seem like an appropriate bracket here

driving home one evening
I heard myself say: "I'd like to encounter
the soul of Allen Ginsberg"
as if it wasn't me who said it
I don't go around saying that

And so then again:
"I'd like to meet
the soul of Allen Ginsberg"
to see if it sounds funny – if not to assess
the weight and feasibility

and once more, I say it, at the red light,
letting the rational mind
and desire, circle each other
like dogs in the park
sniffing at possibilities of a union –
maybe I'll have a dream
or meet someone who'll remind me of him?

that was half-year ago, and nothing
was heard or seen of Allen
but today
as I am writing down this poem
I find myself sharing the table
with Jack Hirschman
felt hat pulled way down, scribbling kabbalistic on shreds
of paper,
upstairs  at the City Lights bookstore –

I know his face from the back-covers
and so, introduced myself
an hour ago, at a coffee shop across the street
and here we're again, in a few minutes
we'll head downstairs for David Meltzer's reading
we both came here for

I hope Jack doesn't think
I'm stalking him

## The Second Place

"that second place we went to on the fifth floor
I really learned something
the guy was speaking almost
my language and it felt so good" –
holding her hand,
he's recounting less
a memory than vision breaking
through – what? not exactly silence
or stupor or the thing of being very old –

they each have long
nails, long grey hair
each holds an identical small black plastic bag

her eyes stay closed all through this
I doubt she is awake
in a way we can understand
only nodding because of the rickety
subway rhythm variations
but as he speaks
her foot is tapping
here and there
often enough
to provide an unmistakable counterpoint

## Palo Alto Sketch

        empty plastic cups
        on a four-wheel cart

    mothers with strollers

a folded white-board on wheels
parked over to the side

      I imagine leaving
imagine a scandal
            a woman pulls on the locked door, gives up
            goes off
old man with a walker

     "do you work here"
        this is work
            the silence
               immobility

three boys rush in, each carrying a bag
    as big as himself

## Ennoblement

what ennobles her?
this opportunity to watch
her own mind go places otherwise unavailable
foreign places, foreign sensations
belonging to a different set of knowing

pushing the sixth decade
in the suburbs, with kids grown up and married,
without career or worry,
disorders long identified and medicated
she wears the feeling
like some regal right
like a sacred confirmation
she lights up
            and feels

# End of the Semester Remarks

a deep reader, your son
        but not an intellectual
there's simply a brooding
        machine somewhere inside him
        shredding everything
that comes into purview
reprocesses it all with soot
none of what he says is original but
it is profound
in a way confusion is profound –
along with its noble source
        and randomness with which it inhabits
and animates
        the aforementioned machinery

I only happened to have fed it
this one semester

# Café "Venetia"

odd to sit at the train station
and wait for no train to come –
hope no train comes altogether – to jolt the lazy paralysis
noise level, people halfsucked
into post-work stupor

sporting a yellowing undershirt:
gave my button-down to the cleaners
was there anyway
"you're not the only one who does it"

I go for it
take off my socks

the illusion of having nowhere
to go feels like swimming
slowly pushing away emptiness
that immediately replenishes itself –
haven't gone swimming in two years
or more?

a homeless man
wanders in with a plastic shopping basket
he's the biggest character here
I can take my socks off
and put them back on all day
won't come close to a homeless black man
with a plastic shopping basket
spilling over his belongings
on the floor of the train station in the second
richest small town in the country

and that, I know, is the end
of the poem:
I have not wondered
        about my poetics
since I started writing this
and going to stop now
so as to nix
the urge, though there must be less
obvious ways to break that addiction


*Palo Alto, Apr 27, 2015*

## Autohistoria
*After Gloria E. Anzaldúa*


I was sitting in my grandmother's kitchen eating fish soup
8 women in colorful skirts shuffle in
they speak with an accent, ask my grandmother
if they could change the baby –
saying they're "Jews from the East"
my grandma offers them fish soup
later I learn about "Romani"
the ultimate other
they tuned into our own otherness
to rob us, my mother explains
but your grandmother's fish soup softened them
they changed the baby and left
from a young age I was cautioned against
getting close to Romani though of course
we, like everyone, sang their songs


until I left Ukraine, I'd never seen anyone with a different skin color
in person, except for the one African student in our Medical Institute –
Soviet initiative to bring communism to Africa
Some kid yelled "chocolate" and ran past him
the man shook his fist


my first month in America I could not distinguish
between my Asian-American classmates


When the Soviet Union collapsed and Ukrainian authorities
rushed to unearth their own history books and literature
I sat in the classroom, sweat running down my back
as we read a crude,  insipid Ukrainian rip-off
of the "Merchant of Venice"
the author used vaguely Yiddish-sounding phrases to fill out the character
my classmates would repeat and snicker
Trying to dodge learning portions of the play by heart
"Tricky people, so tricky" the teacher tells me –

second year in America, in a subway car,
African American man tells me I'm not Jewish
if Moses lived in Egypt, he says, his hair would be curly like this –
I lift my hat: but my hair *is* curly like yours I say– people around us
laughing, typical New York scene,
and we're both laughing too

knowing what I know today I would have agreed with the man
besides, I've grown bald – there goes the proof –
and what of my Slavic grandmother
and others who joined
real and imaginary
all of those who scrubbed their difference
my parents didn't tell me we were Jews till I was eight
and came home from school singing an anti-Semitic ditty

and what's with all these here stories – an attempt to carve
out my own difference? anecdotes, don't
they pale in contrast with those
of others – those who've really suffered?

These are the foundational stories that surface
when I think of my own edges – or rather,
when I think of waking up to certain truths –
                    or trying to lose them?

*

*One day, on the New York subway, I observed myself, as if from the
outside, changing cars to avoid sitting next to a Russian-speaking couple.
I could not stand the sound of the language, could not stand sitting in the
proximity of a world it immediately drew me into. As the walls graffitied
with incomprehensible signatures flashed in the train's window, the question
dislodged itself. Is self-loathing the required toll, exacted from each and every
immigrant by assimilation's demands? Or is it a form of allaying the pain of
breached family connections, innumerable cultural nerves cut loose? Or is it
a nightmarish border police encounter, playing out within the space of my
pre-lingual, fugitive impulses? These questions came back some weeks later,
as I found myself re-recording my voicemail message over a dozen times,
miffed by the traces of my accent, that surfaced each time in a different spot
of that muffled 30 second recording.*

*When it comes to writing, my reflex, by now entirely naturalized, is to edit
out every trace of the mother-tongue. I am not proud of this reflex. These
next few poems are less of an attempt to subvert it than to distract myself
with a bone of self-caricature. Unlike the elegantly bipedal Biblical parables
– planted in the text in neat parallel structures – Russian proverbial
speech of my childhood is hobbled, fragmentary, absurd, and, above all,
disdainfully sarcastic. "To walk seven miles to slurp compote," you say about
someone engaged in hard work that, in your estimation, culminates in
little to no gain. Insight, or wisdom, is not a relevant dimension in these
parables. Pithy and seemingly idiotic sayings are, instead, rooted in the
delivery's pathos, or bathos, or even just in a rhythmic retaliation against
whatever is irritating the speaker at any given moment. "It is better to be
rich and healthy, than to be poor and sick," my father would often say, with
revelatory airs, and a concealed smirk. Allowing these sayings to exist in
another language is like "trying to go to two market places with your one
butt-cheek," which perhaps is a worthwhile way to travel, for a poet. In the
poems below, tidbits of Russian proverbial language appear as lines, titles,
and epigraphs.*

*

## One Year Plan

*"before we get going,*
*        let's all lay down"*

>                    everyone must be buttoned
>                    to the top a-la chairman Mao

chest hair! through the linen shirt
the subject hangs
clanging
        convivially as we waltz –
waltz all night
        and how wonderful the weather!

>                in the middle of these nameless steppes
>                wind bends grasses perpendicularly, lets go:
>                agrarian corn-heaven
>                        (each kernel as big as a wisdom tooth –
>                        and glistening, we waltz

waltz all night)

we tumble
        our victory
                assured by new coughing
                refrigeration facilities and stolen light-
                        stolen light-
                                        stolen light-
                                                bulbs
                that will last through the rest
                        of this unforgettable year

## Same Ass but View Sideways

mirrors of fat,
      circle fatefully
      evading the spoon
            "let me tell"

"this weather, it's very deceptive"

"that's alright, it's not what gentile women
love us for"

"one day they remind you
              who – "

yes yes, this world, etc.:
Pushkin, Mandelshtam, the radio

in these pants?

             what you know
             is every buttock
in town, tapped each one lovingly
on public transportation
with your bags of groceries
      the provider!
"they" spend their dough
drinking but we:  invite relatives and talk, talk
we talk how we eat, in
          circles, blowing

## Banya

Age 5, first time at the public bathhouse, banya,

I thought everyone's penis

    looked like a miniature accordion


"usage"      "music"


my grandfather tersely explained

# Memoir

my aunt's friend worked at a meat factory
that mass produced secret kielbasas, salamis, cured meats
inaccessible to the general public
   and because there were eyes
and ears everywhere, on the phone, with my aunt,
the friend used code:
       "This week, I have what's hurting
               your husband"
          meaning, fresh liver
      and a meeting would be arranged


          my uncle's
liver must have swelled every time with the signifier's burden –
professor of Marxist philosophy
      in our provincial university –
when he heard a joke he liked
instead of laughing, he'd make a pained smile and say:
"so, is that how it is?"

## Checkers in Reverse

here is the cosmos of translation
of the word "poddavki"

which refers to the way Russians
play checkers
in reverse, the "advanced way":

goal being to lose
position yourself so as to be destroyed

*the appetite comes when you start eating*
the old proverb goes

and because capturing is mandatory
you can feed your opponent
      his miserable victory

the real pro's
      play poddavki
            alone

\*\*\*

*I've read enough Kafka to know that our visions are often and inevitably constituted of metaphors drawn from work-life. At some point, the corporate structure – its hierarchies and reward systems – could seep into one's theology. The following two sets of poems document work-life at two separate jobs, both of which, I'm glad to say, are now far behind me.*

## Lunch Break Reflections

if the last thirteen years amounted to breaking
even, making the rent,
      I did live between
      the cracks, in a minimized
browser at the bottom of the screen
you could say I was reconciling two sides
          of some primordial balance
sheet, whole in my lack
      of options
perhaps I've been answering
some unknowable need of purification

          life has not materialized
as fulfillment
as revelation

and yet
and yet

# At the Annual Review Meeting

in the middle of the meeting I
suddenly remember my father spinning the egg
teaching me how to tell if it's raw or
cooked without cracking & I can't
remember which is which but suddenly this
domesticated Ukrainian
      roulette is what I'm willing
to stake my whole workday on

a decade of workdays

## Clerical Prophecy

like everything else I learned outside
of training sessions
                           & instruction manuals
            this too I overheard
                in the burr of the shredding machine
          in voicemails muffled
behind closed office doors
              I heard all
about having to, needing to
about having to, needing to
          carry yourself like two mythic cups
             coffee and water
                   alternating currents
                  of the clerical prophecy

# Meet and Greet

when people pass by her mid-floor cubicle
she introduces them
      to pictures of her cats
      Zack and Renee
and a large dried bouquet: got married this year!
photo of her husband
is there too, in profile,
      concealed under a large
      baseball hat

## Scenario Analysis


lets say in the middle of a coffee break –

– come on all day is a coffee break –

at some point, drinking coffee, inside the cubicle
    you cry out
        silent and desperate
            & your cry reaches –
      & blossoms there
       & you sort of realize it
       & pile in more
         requests

       also, answer


            an email, or over
       the cube wall, colleague's call
      or the thought
         simply wonders, well then
    isn't this other stuff –
      the distractions, mere
      dust from keyboard's interstices –
      funneling
        upwards

    all this, now on record?

who's going to want to open
the door to your cry ever again

## Clicks

before the workday officially started
we're both already there
chatting
via instant chat
she sits a few cubicles across but
we're both more at ease, each with apparitions of other
as terse phrase-strings –
"doing ok"   "checking in on…"
we can faintly hear
the other clicking buttons
faster and slower   probably erasing something   stopping to think
convivial, shy

## Comparative Religion

in the office bathroom
as we're washing our hands
co-worker tells me he composed a new holiday song
about Xmas and Hanukkah:
 "8 times more presents!
Jesus got nothing on Jahweh"
is the chorus –

"Jahweh"

bounces
around bathroom walls

I blow my nose
not out of disrespect –
got allergies, didn't sleep –
he stops singing
face in the tissue, I motion: keep going
he doesn't
"some people are offended" he says
"I'm putting down Jesus like that
guess I'm a bad Christian"
and as I hold the door for him, adds:
"gonna send this to Adam Sandler
that guy is a fucking god!"

## In the Red

when you work at a small company
and generate less revenue
than your income
it is as if your whole existence is unjustified
you're the wet rag sinking the firm
deeper into the Red
Sea – whole life dangling
above the waters like pharaoh's scattered loot

# Data Center Demolition

we come and it's already dead, powered
down or maybe still flickering, waiting suspended
for the final round of electricians

stacked servers
are the ones you'd call the living center
      of this warehouse-sized space
growling, heated mass dreaming up
transcendence
as a "cloud"

off they go, these servers, in the scrapper
barely worth their material's weight
prematurely ancient

we're going after the machines in the locked cabinets
mostly forgotten, the Uninterrupted
Power Supply that kicks in when the grid
is down – once in the data center's whole lifetime? – if that –
uninterrupted
              power
struggling to hedge its own fragility
we package them with cardboard corners
wrap in blankets and saran, ship them off
where they'll be stripped
of wires, their parts harvested
and later reused for replacement and maintenance

## In a Day's Work

the truck is there but where's the wire
where's wire at
call the accounting lady again –
stop being so nice all the time
instead of being nice, be clear
need wire to send wire
must sell in order to buy
the trucker will charge us extra
the workmen will charge
call my guy about his guy
did they anyway load everything –
everything? –
lengthwise, put her lengthwise there so all fits
and where's the wire everyone approved
can't believe it till you see
call the bank? no
call the lady again?
call call call do something else so you don't freak out
the trucker's boss is on the line
is the truck ready to cut loose?
what if I took it out of your commission?
what if this was your money?

## Lovers of Used Things

we're not brokers:
I see our role as godlike
planting desire
sourcing hope in the guise
of a bargain –
products, buyers and sellers both
"anything else you looking for?"
sometimes in the middle of a deal
they stop answering email
and phone – we call it "going dark"
but eventually all come back
as if nothing happened, bidding, stretching,
and we let them because one day they'll pull through
and then the game's reset
back to the start

## Bargaining

"where you need to be at" they
ask meaning: how much
meaning: where do we begin
our little dance
of who's-more-desperate
game, in which the cards
are your life's circumstances:
late with rent this week – anniversary coming up –
the forces are moving through every sentence of
you
where you
need to be at
they ask as if leaning
over a map
pointing, at some unmarked destination on this odyssey

## Winter 2013/2014

I may remember this as the year
everything went to shit
when I stopped writing, writhing
when I understood our faux middle
class status, the poverty,
and paid much interest
on maxed out credit cards
and worked and worked
and watched TV and drank a lot
days coagulated  many emails
went unanswered
some collections letters
it's harder to make friends in your mid 30's
easier to fade away into your family home
family apartment
I may remember this as the coldest winter ever
and revolution in Ukraine
and my daughter's first months on this planet
salivating smiles in the middle of the night

the image of multiple worlds that the mind can't seem to interlace
I may have even thought of them
as divine
not almighty or merciful
but a living pile
inside some lost pagan fishnet
dragged by a force unknown to itself

# Change of Weather

who lost who
first –
an exotic
dancer did she
loosen
her hold, loosen her keep
in the kitchen
of a self-
help-course-hosting
old Philly building
she did not want
to be tied
down to an ex-con
salesman
and his Orthodox family
she didn't lose
faith she didn't
have to begin
or end any of it she simply hated
his gastrological
tract, he lost
the prescription
he lost the real
body instead they watched
imaginary shape
dancing, rubbing up
against a future he imagined –
yes, she stopped,
lost her spot on
*that* stage as he paid
her bills it's terribly
real, this story, I lost
my cool and left
the office I couldn't

listen to him retell
the story again into
another ear across
the phone line
it teetered on finale
he kept saying whore
kept saying love
and I kept thinking
I bet she could really dance but
isn't she kind of too old
for that and wasn't that self-
help course he met her at
a very middle class sort of
entertainment, gut
spilling as backup
generator of meaning
and wasn't she half-
Jewish? We didn't lose
our range of capabilities
as people in this arid, upward
pushing moment I thought
I'm so lucky to breathe in
spring, been a cold and lonely
winter my kids are driving me
vertically up some invisible
wall of fulfillment and we lost
the business of paying bills
on time, my business,
is to walk the straight line into financial salvation
and this guy across the desk is an ex-
con about to become single
with his ring back and her suitcase packed
she didn't want to come
to his Orthodox family's Seder,
didn't want gastro-
logical commitment maybe she
wanted to dance again she wanted

the lost dance she couldn't tell between
it and other lesser sorts of loss
maybe it had nothing
to do with spring or Pesach
or money or pot he was
imprisoned for but it was
a blue body of many arms
hugging all of us at the same time
blue body to whom spring
mattered not at all but loss
was its air it both
breathed in and exhaled
blue body that lost its spot
at the Seder, wasn't spoken about,
but was there, exiting, girded
in mythic history, I don't want
to praise or prove anything
defensively conspiring
exit strategies out of a big truth
of winter lost to rocking
the baby and pacifying the burning
brain and pot does unblock love
and the love seeping
slips out but it is blue
and it is bruised and I
attribute it all to this new line
of work, this business
I've been involved in this year
legitimate but how bruised
and bruising and real
I will look back at it
as lost time but is it?
timeless in its blueness
in its lost ambition and debts
I've been calling it Egypt this
whole past month but
Egypt's got its own problems

doesn't need my bad vibes
and financial anxiety
on top of its own shortage
of food supply to say nothing
of the fundamentalism


Apr 2014

## Glossary

**4 cups:** as per Passover tradition of self-liberation via four mandatory glasses of wine during the Seder - each cup stands in for a new level of redemption.

**Baal Shem:** semi-mythic, shamanic founder of Hassidism, popularized into coherence by Martin Buber.

**Chazzan:** cantor/performer, counter-argument against language's materiality, as per Ornette Coleman's comment on Yossele Rosenblatt's singing: "You can't find those notes. Those are not 'notes.' They don't exist."

**Gematria:** a system of correspondences, operating on the assumption that each letter has a numeric value and that words/phrases which happen to add up to the same sum are mystically connected. See Jerome Rothenberg's "Gematria," a breakthrough recasting of the mystical interpretive practice into a method of poetic composition.

**Jahweh:** ...

**Midrash:** ancient poetic hermeneutics

**Nigun:** bent wordless chant, incantatory echolocation

**Shalom Aleichem:** Friday night song to welcome the shabbes angels

**Shul:** synagogue but warmer, older, imaginary